RAISED BED GARDENING

A DIY Guide To Raised Bed Gardening

STEVE MUFIA

Text Copyright © 2018 STEVE MUFIA

All rights reserved. No part of this guide may be reproduced in any form without permission in writing from the publisher except in the case of brief quotations embodied in critical articles or reviews.

Legal & Disclaimer

The content or information contained in this book is not designed to replace or take the place of any form of medical or professional advice; and is not meant to replace the need for independent medical, financial, legal or other professional advice or services, as may be required. The content or information in this book has been provided for educational and entertainment purposes only.

The content or information contained in this book is from sources deemed reliable, and it is accurate to the best of the author's knowledge, information and belief. However, the author cannot guarantee its accuracy and validity and cannot be held liable for any errors and/or omissions. Further changes are periodically made to this book as and when needed. Where appropriate and necessary, you must consult a professional (including but not limited to your doctor, attorney, financial advisor or such other professional advisor) before using any of the suggested remedies, techniques, or information in this book.

Upon using the content or information contained in this book, you agree not to hold the author responsible for any damages, costs, and expenses, including any legal fees potentially resulting from the application of any of the information provided in this book. This disclaimer applies to any loss, damages or injury caused by the use and application, whether directly or indirectly, of any advice or information presented, whether for breach of contract, tort, negligence, personal injury, criminal intent, or under any other cause of action.

You agree to accept all risks of using the information presented inside this book.

You agree that by continuing to read this book, where appropriate and/or necessary, you shall consult a professional (including but not limited to your doctor, attorney, or financial advisor or such other advisor as needed) before using any of the suggested remedies, techniques, or information in this book.

Table of Contents

Introduction.. 7

Chapter 1 10

HOW TO BUILD A RAISED BED 10

Chapter 2 18

TYPES OF RAISED BED GARDENS 18

    KEYHOLE RAISED BEDS.................................. 18

    MAKING A RECTANGULAR RAISED BED......... 29

    HOW TO BUILD RAISED BED FROM BALES OF STRAW... 34

    OTHER TYPES OF EASY TO CONSTRUCT RAISED BED... 36

Chapter 3 40

RAISED BED GARDEN DESIGNS 40

Chapter 4 45

TOP FIVE VEGETABLES THAT GROW BEST IN RAISED BED GARDENS 45

Chapter 5 50

TIPS FOR RAISED BED GARDENING.................... 50

    TEN TIPS FOR RAISED BED GARDENING 51

    How Many Raised Beds Can You Have? 54

Chapter 6 57

BENEFITS OF RAISED BED GARDENING.............. 57

Conclusion 65

Check Out Other Books..................................... 67

Introduction

Raised-bed gardening is a type of gardening in which the soil is fashioned in three-to-four-foot-wide (1.0–1.2 m) beds. These beds are constructed above the natural terrain. The beds can be of any shape or length. The formed soil is raised on top of the surrounding soil (about six inches to waist-high), and sometimes, it is enclosed by a frame usually made of rock, wood, or concrete blocks, and may be enhanced with compost.

The vegetable plants are spaced in geometric outlines much closer together than in usual row gardening. The spacing is such that by the time the vegetables are completely grown, their leaves just hardly touch each other, forming a microclimate in which weed growth is concealed and moisture is preserved. Raised beds supply an array of benefits:

They lengthen the planting season,

They can decrease weeds when arranged and planted correctly, and

They lessen the call for the use of poor native soil.

As a gardener, you would not step on the raised beds. This makes the soil to be compacted and the roots don't have a difficult time growing. The close plant spacing idea and the use of compost usually leads to higher yields with raised beds when compared to the usual row gardening.

Waist-high raised beds allow older people and physically disabled individuals to grow vegetables without the need to bend over to take care of them.

Raised beds are useful for the growth of multifaceted agriculture systems that uses many of the principles and systems of permaculture. They can be efficiently utilized to manage erosion, recycle and preserve water and nutrients by building them along contour lines on slopes. This as well makes more space accessible for serious crop production. They can be formed over wide areas, using more than a few commonly available tractor-drawn implements and professionally maintained, planted and harvested with the use of hand tools.

This type of gardening is well matched with square foot gardening and companion planting.

Circular raised beds that have a path to the center (a slice of the circle cut out) are referred to as keyhole gardens. Frequently, the center has a chimney of sorts constructed with sticks and then lined with feedbags or grasses that give room to the water placed at the center to flow out into the soil and reach the plant roots.

This guide will show you how you can make raised bed gardens easily with accessible materials.

Chapter 1

HOW TO BUILD A RAISED BED

Before building the bed, you have to consider some pertinent factors.

1. Location of the raised bed

The first step in planning a raised bed is deciding where it will be located. Site selection and plant selection go hand in hand. Many vegetables, ornamentals and herbs require a lot of sunlight; a bed for these plants should be located where it will receive full sun. If that is not possible, select a site that receives morning rather than afternoon sun. If only shady sites are available, try growing cool season vegetables that tolerate shade, such as broccoli, cabbage and lettuce.

In addition, some ornamental plants do best in partial shade. In windy regions, place beds where they are protected from prevailing winds by fences, buildings or other structures. Beds should not be located in frost pockets or where air circulation is poor because fungal diseases often develop where there is little airflow.

2. Drainage

A raised bed should drain well because soil that remains very wet will deprive plant roots of oxygen.

Also, plant diseases develop more easily under wet conditions. Good drainage is especially important in vegetable beds.

The soil and the location determine how well a raised bed will drain. If the bed contains clay soil, it should be amended with at least one-third by volume of coarse sand, organic matter or a coarse grade of perlite to improve drainage.

Do not locate a bed in a marshy area where it will sit in water. Construct landscape beds so that they slope about 2 percent (a ¼-inch drop per foot of horizontal distance) away from any structures, or away from the center of the bed.

Sometimes it is necessary to install special drains; determine this during the planning stage.

Drain tiles or septic line tubing can be extended through the length of the bed and through the walls at either end to create a drainage channel. Normally, one line every 4 to 6 feet is sufficient. Another way is to dig a trench in the desired direction of water flow (from the bed to a lower elevation), lay 3 to 4 inches of coarse stone in the trench, and then lay tiles or perforated tubing made of clay, concrete or plastic in the center of the trench. Cover the trench with more coarse stone and then soil.

The French drain, another alternative, is simply a narrow trench filled with coarse stone leading from a poorly drained area to a lower elevation.

3. Design

A raised bed should blend with its surroundings. The bed's design may be formal or informal, depending on its shape and the kind of edging chosen. A rectangular bed edged with a low brick wall, and filled with yaupon (Ilex vomitoria) or boxwood (Buxus spp) pruned into straight hedges or topiaries, has a formal look that might be appropriate in the front of a house. An irregularly shaped perennial border tucked behind a dry stone wall is less formal but could be attractive almost anywhere in the landscape. A vegetable garden has an informal look that works best in private areas of the yard. The size of the bed should be kept in proportion to the space around it.

A raised bed does not have to be very deep to be effective. Eight to 12 inches is usually adequate. If drainage is a problem, or if the plants you are growing prefer drier soil, the bed could be taller and filled with a porous growing medium. Vegetable beds should be 12 to 18 inches deep. The material used to edge a raised bed should be stable, durable and attractive. The edging gives the bed its "look" within the landscape. It also establishes the outline of the bed and holds the soil in place. Edging may be as simple as metal strips, railroad ties or landscape timbers, or as intricate as a mortared brick or stone. A crested bed is one in which the soil is simply mounded from the edges of the bed to the centre; it may or may not have an edging.

Metal edging comes in 8 to 10-foot lengths, is easy to install, and is convenient for edging curved beds. However, it can rust with time, and unless plantings overflow the bed or the edging is camouflaged with a more aesthetic material, it may not be as attractive as you would like.

Ties and timbers can be laid singly or in layers and have a rustic appearance. Railroad ties treated with creosote do not appear to pose any health problems because most of the creosote has leached away. There is some controversy about using treated landscape timbers, but studies have shown that any compounds that leach out are well within safe levels established by the US EPA, both in growing media and in harvested produce. If you are concerned about using treated timbers, line the inside of the bed walls with polyethylene, roofing felt or similar materials to form a protective barrier. Stone walls make interesting beds, and can be constructed with cracks and openings for creative plantings.

4. Critter Control

One of the perks of having a raised bed in your yard is the possibility of controlling the wildlife that munches on and destroys your prized plants. Have you ever grown big, red tomatoes, letting them get redder and riper on the vine, only to go outside one morning to find that some discriminating creature has taken a bite out of it, probably spit it out, then gone on to see what else is being offered at your backyard buffet?

To keep your beds low maintenance, choose plants that are disease resistant and are not attractive to animals and insects.

Maintain a healthy garden by using fertile soil, the right amount of fertilizer, irrigation, and sun or shade. Group together plants with similar needs.

Before resorting to pesticides (often a last resort), try using organic methods, like barriers, a good blast from the hose, or sprays made from non-toxic household products.

Gophers, Moles and Ground Squirrels

These underground miscreants can tunnel

through the soil, munching on bulbs and shoots. If this scenario occurs in your raised bed, place root balls in wire cages or line planting holes with barriers of hardware cloth.

Snails and Slugs

Use 3-inch-high copper bands to enclose vegetable and flower beds. Unbelievably, the copper emits a small electrical shock when a snail or slug touches it, making it retreat (not enough to kill it).

Another method is to fill a shallow bowl with beer, dig a small hole so that the bowl's lip is flush with the top of the soil. Snails and slugs are attracted to the beer, will go swimming in it, and drown.

Flying and Crawling Insects

Protect vegetables leaves from flying and crawling insects by covering them with gauze. Find it at garden centers or online retailers.

Once these factors are in place, you can now take a breath of fresh air and get ready to construct your bed.

Are you ready?

I'm sure you are.

Let us discuss on the different types of raised beds.

Chapter 2

TYPES OF RAISED BED GARDENS

KEYHOLE RAISED BEDS

The keyhole garden is a 2-meter wide circular raised garden with a keyhole-shaped indentation on one side that was developed in Lesotho by the Consortium for Southern Africa Food Security Emergency (C-SAFE).

The indentation allows the gardener to add uncooked vegetable scraps, water and manure into a composting basket that sits in the centre of the bed. This allows composting materials to be added to the basket throughout the growing season to provide nutrients for the plants.

The upper layer of soil is hilled up against the centre basket so the soil slopes gently down from the center to the sides. Most keyhole gardens rise one meter above the ground and have walls made of stone. The stone wall not only gives the garden its form, but helps trap moisture within the bed.

Before we delve into how you can make this bed yourself, let us discuss on the general equipment needed for any raised bed.

Supplies to Build Raised Garden Beds
- Lumber
- Power saw
- Carpenter's square
- Carpenter's level
- Drill, drill bits
- 4" screws, 1" screws
- Metal braces

- Landscape fabric
- Tape measure
- Wheelbarrow (for transporting compost)
- Trowel
- Steel rake
- Safety goggles
- Face mask
- Gloves
- Post-hole digger (optional)
- Small pruning saw (optional)
- Old lumber for temporary bracing (optional)
- Flat stones for shims (optional)
- Wood preservative (optional, to make the wood last longer)
- Cedar and redwood are popular types of wood for raised beds. They are naturally rot-resistant.

STEPS IN MAKING A SINGLE RAISED KEYHOLE BED

- **Step 1**

Mark out a circle where you want to site your keyhole bed. As mentioned, the size of your bed will depend on a number of factors. The available space for cultivation, your mobility and reach, the materials you have available, and the number of species of plant you wish to grow will all play a part in deciding how large to make your bed.

As a rough guide, however, work on a bed with a diameter of around 6 feet. This will give enough room to grow a number of different plants, and allow you to reach all parts of the bed for harvesting.

You can mark the circle by using stones placed on the ground or by digging the marked areas and placing sticks around it held by a twine.

- **Step 2**

Mark out the keyhole access path. This is where you will stand to reach the bed and where you will site the central composting pile. If using the 6-foot diameter circle, mark a center circle of around a foot across, and then mark a path — either straight or in a wedge shape depending on your mobility need – to the edge of the main circle.

- **Step 3**

Construct the outer wall of your keyhole bed (remembering to leave the access path open). One of the benefits of this style of garden bed is that you can construct it from any number of recycled materials, as you are essentially building a retaining wall to hold the growing medium. Broken bricks, rocks, timber or metal are all options, depending on what sort of recycled material you can source. You might even consider using discarded plastic bottles filled with sand and bound with clay, as a way to make use of waste products that do not biodegrade. Any material is feasible as long as it is strong enough to hold in the growing medium. However, different materials will create different microclimates within and around the bed (for instance, rocks retain heat more than timber) but this can provide a wider variety of growing opportunities.

- **Step 4**

Create the center compost provider. This is a wire mesh tube into which kitchen scraps and other green composting material is placed, providing the keyhole bed with a constant supply of nutrients and moisture. Roll up a piece of wire mesh around four feet tall into a tube about 1 foot in diameter and place in the center of your bed.

- **Step 5**

Fill in the keyhole bed with layers of compostable material. Ideally, you want a ratio of about three to one of brown to green materials. Your brown materials could include fallen leaves, straw, sawdust, newspapers, cardboard and pruning from the garden. Green material may include scraps from the kitchen, composted animals manure, and grass clippings. Water each layer of material well as you go.

At the top, adda few inches of potting soil and some compost. The heat generated by this layering of material will serve to break it down and turn it into rich soil.

- **Step 6**

Fill the center tube with green composting material. Paper scraps from the kitchen, coffee grinds and manure can all go in here. Keep it topped up regularly with material to ensure that the soil in the bed remains high in nutrients. In combination with natural rainfall events, it will supply sufficient water to keep the plants happy (only water the bed and center compost pile if the plants are visibly in need of extra moisture). This centerpiece also promotes strong root growth in the plants sited in the keyhole bed, as their roots are attracted to the nutrient rich area and so penetrate more deeply into the soil.

- **Step 7**

Plant your keyhole bed. The species you choose will depend upon your personal taste and the climate conditions on your site, but it can be useful to approach planting your keyhole bed as a zone system in miniature.

For instance, in the area closest to the center you could plant fast-growing species that you would harvest often, such as lettuce, salad greens, and herbs.

The next circle out would comprise plants that you harvest slightly less often, such as tomatoes, peppers and peas, while in the zone beyond those you could plant slower-growing crops like potatoes, carrots and onions. Some of these plants are, however, not completely recommended for keyhole garden as you would see.

It is also worth thinking of the bed as a guild, so combining species that benefit one another through their proximity – be it providing shade, fixing nitrogen, repelling insects, and so on – can prove very beneficial. Placing taller plants on the edge of the bed can help protect lower-lying plants from damage by sun or wind, and can generate microclimates within the bed.

- **Step 8**

Harvest your crops when they ripen, and return any scraps from the kitchen that result from their use to the center compost pile. This will ensure a sustainable keyhole garden bed that is energy efficient and productive.

PREFERRED CROPS FOR KEYHOLE GARDENS

Root Crops -   Carrot, Onion, Beetroot, Radish, Turnips, Garlic.

Leafy Crops -   Spinach, Swiss chard, Lettuce, Rape, Mustard spinach, Herbs.

CROPS NOT RECOMMENDED FOR KEYHOLE GARDENS

Tomatoes, Peppers, Chilies, PeaS, Potatoes

Cabbage, Eggplant, Maize, Beans, Squash

HOW TO MAINTAIN THE KEYHOLE GARDEN

Watering
- The garden should be watered regularly so that the garden soil is moist.
- Use clean water on the topsoil.
- Water from washing hands, laundry, or dishes is poured into the basket. The thatch and the composting in the basket will clean the water.

Basket

- Uncooked vegetable scraps, dry manure, eggshells, and compost are added to the basket. These replenish the soil.
- The basket will decompose within 1 or 2 years and should be replaced.
- The garden wall near the basket can be pulled away, allowing gardeners to remove the old basket and replace it.

Soil

- Dry manure and topsoil should be replenished in the garden so that it does not become sapped of its fertility.

Garden construction

- Over time, the garden may lose its nutrients, and vegetables stop growing well. You then need to rebuild the garden. This is usually done every 4–5 years.

BENEFITS OF THE KEYHOLE GARDEN

Soil enrichment

- The layers of organic materials decompose over time, adding nutrients to the soil.
- The central composting basket continuously replenishes the soil.

Labor saving technology
- The soil re-nourishment and moisture retention reduce the amount of time required to maintain the garden.
- The garden shape makes it more accessible to sick or elderly gardeners.

Moisture retention
- The layers soak up moisture, so the garden requires less water to remain moist.

Low-cost design
- All construction materials should be readily available (at no cost) to gardeners.
- Gardeners might need to purchase seeds for planting, however.

MAKING A RECTANGULAR RAISED BED

Size

You can use your desired size. A popular bed size is 4 feet x 4 feet. Other common sizes are 4x8 and 3x8.

Depth

This bed is about ten inches deep, but you can make a raised bed as shallow or deep as needed. Consider the root system of the plants you're growing and the method of gardening you're using. Some methods, such as square foot gardening, require less depth than others do.

Materials

Choose a rot-resistant material for the frame of the raised bed. Also, if you are growing food for eating, avoid any treated lumber. If you have cedar logs, that will be great. Use them. Definitely use the resources at hand if possible. Stone is another possibility. Cedar and redwood are popular types of wood for raised beds, as they are naturally rot-resistant.

Once you have your dimensions and your materials, lay cardboard on the ground on the site of the raised bed. If weeds are an issue, consider using 1/8" hardware cloth (woven wire mesh) as the bottom of the bed as well. This is essential if you want to grow strawberries in an area full of quack grass and other heavy weeds that would take over a strawberry bed.

Then, cut and fasten the four sides together in place on the site of the bed. The specifics of this will depend on the material you have chosen. For wood, use a 2x2 piece on the interior corner and screw each side into that.

Covering the bottom of the bed

Adjust the hardware cloth and use a staple gun to staple it all around the bottom of the raised bed. This seals out weeds, tunnelling animals and insects.

If you want to apply a finish or sealer to your wood, you can do that at this stage. Stick with natural finishes such as linseed oil for food crops.

Lining the Sides

Depending on the material you used to construct your raised bed, you may need to use weed block to line the sides of the bed as well as the bottom.

Fill With Soil

This is the fun part! You get to fill the raised bed

with your soil or soil mix. However, what do you use? In addition, how much?

The quantity of soil needed to fill your raised bed can be determined by calculating the volume. A four foot by 8-foot bed, one-foot deep, has a volume of 32 cubic feet.

This is obtained by multiplying the length by width by height to get volume, making sure all the measurements are in the same unit of measure (feet).

Many bagged soils and mixes give their volume in cubic feet. This makes it easy to calculate how much to buy to fill a raised bed.

If you wish to build raised beds on a larger scale, you can use an online converter to change volume to cubic yards, which is the number you will need when you call local nurseries and soil suppliers for your order. However, if you own one or can borrow someone's pickup truck, you can pick the soil up yourself, saving often-hefty delivery fees.

What to fill it with? Topsoil is a simple choice that works for most situations. Another option is to choose a soil mix, such as the 1/3 peat moss, 1/3 compost, 1/3 vermiculite mix used in square foot gardening. There are also some soil/compost industries that offer premade mixes specifically for raised beds.

If you're making a mix, spread a tarp, and don't try it on a windy day. Use rakes and shovels to combine the ingredients, mixing very well. With a helper, lift the tarp and dump the soil into the raised bed.

It is time to plant

Now, it is time to get to the most fun and satisfying step after all your hard work building a raised bed. Plant whatever it is you're growing!

Reap the benefits of few weeds and the perfect soil mix when you use a raised bed to grow vegetables or berries. If you want to grow as much food as possible in a small urban or suburban space, raised beds can be a huge ally in the effort.

HOW TO BUILD RAISED BED FROM BALES OF STRAW

You can build a fast, easy raised bed from bales of straw. The idea is easy: You create a bed frame with the bales then fill up the space inside with a blend of premium quality potting soil and compost. A raised bed made with straw bales is a convenient and cheap way to create your first garden or add to the growing space you already have.

Bales of wheat straw, oat straw, or alfalfa straw would work best for this type of raised bed. Hay bales can also work, but they have many seeds, which may become a bother. Go for bales bound with synthetic twine, which won't break down.

During the first growing season, the bales will settle and decompose a little, adding nutrients to the thriving garden in it. A raised bed made with straw bales can last a few growing seasons, depending on where you reside. (It will decompose faster in warmer, damper climates). As an additional bonus, when the straw begins to break down, it will start to generate a rich soil you can use for future planting.

Step 1

Plan your bed shape and size, and buy the number of bales you need for the planned shape and size.

Step 2

Position the bales in a square or rectangle. Fit them together firmly.

Step 3

Fill up the bed with soil. You can use half-potting mix and half compost.

Step 4

Assemble a soaker hose over the soil, and affix it to your primary hose and spigot.

Step 5

Plant your bed with vegetables, flowers, and herbs.

OTHER TYPES OF EASY TO CONSTRUCT RAISED BED

Raised garden beds boost up vegetables over potentially waterlogged grounds. Not all gardeners deal with a high water table, but there are other good motives behind planting in raised beds:

- They are less difficult to protect from encroaching grass than the ground level beds.
- Raised soil warms earlier in spring and drains faster after raining.
- Soil does not become compacted since you don't step on the growing area.

- Raised beds provide straightforward access for planting, thinning, weeding, and harvest.

The following five raised beds are created from different materials, explained below. Each of these beds measures around 4-feet by 8 feet; you can regulate the dimensions to go well with your needs. However, keep in mind that anything wider than 4 feet will be more complicated to maintain. Try filling beds with a generous blend of about two parts soil and one part compost.

Wattle

Drive 2-foot lengths of rebar into the ground about the perimeter of the bed, spacing them around 16 inches apart and leaving 10 inches of the rebar bare above ground. Cut lengthy, straight lengths of tree or shrub branches, about a 1/2 inch in diameter. Interlace the sticks or "wattle" all the way through the vertical rebar, basket style; trim the ends at the bed corners as required. Once the bedsides have gotten to the top of the rebar, curve 2-foot sticks in half and thrust them into the ground above the woven wattle, holding the sticks in place. Fix the sides in this way every few feet. Line the sides of the bed with burlap to prevent soil from sifting through the wattle.

To construct a 4-foot by 8-foot bed, you will need 18 pieces of rebar. Each should be 24-inches long; a strip of burlap almost 18 inches wide and 24-feet long; and about 100 long, bendable sticks.

Logs

Use straight logs nearly a foot in diameter to form the bed edges. Logs of shorter diameter can be stacked. To evade having to move huge logs, line up shorter firewood-length sections.

To construct a 4-foot by 8-foot bed, you will require two 7-foot logs for the sides and two 4-foot logs for the ends.

Concrete Blocks

Position concrete blocks with open ends facing up to draw the raised bed. The openings can be stacked with soil and utilized as planting pockets for small herbs or edible flowers.

To design a 4-foot by 8-foot bed, you should have 16 blocks, each measuring 8-by-8-by-16 inches.

Planks + Rebar

This bed can be built with leftover lumber of nearly any dimension, as long as the wood is not treated. Put the planks on edge with short lengths of rebar driven into the ground every 2 or 3 feet.

To construct a 4-foot by 8-foot bed, you should get a two 2-by-12 plank 8-feet long, two 2-by-12 planks 4-feet long, and 12 pieces of rebar, each 24 inches long.

Sandbags

With the use of the long, slim bags of sand that are sold as traction sand, outline a bed. Load the bags high all the way about the bed.

To erect a 4-foot by 8-foot bed, get 20 sandbags.

Chapter 3

RAISED BED GARDEN DESIGNS

- **Potager Raised Bed Design**

A raised bed potager, or kitchen garden, shows the arranged, formal design these beds can bring to a setting. Easy wood frames built from rot-resistant lumber supplies years of rising success. Raised beds give themselves to demanding gardening methods such as inter-planting, succession planting, and square-foot gardening.

- **Colourful Raised Bed**

When raised beds are created with UV-stable polypropylene, they infuse a landscape with beautiful colour all year-round. Plastic beds supply long life and don't deteriorate like wood can. Just make sure you choose materials that are UV-stable to put off rapid breakdown by sun exposure. This design also comes with easy interlocking corners.

- **Stone Beds Last Forever**

Stacked stones provide a long-lasting bed edging that doesn't rot despite contact with wet soil. Stones might have a formal arrangement, like the stacked slate raised bed. The stone absorbs heat and radiates it into soil inside the raised bed, allowing you to plant sooner in spring and let crops grow longer in fall.

- **Informal Stone Raised Bed**

A casual stone raised bed design showcases individual boulders loaded and fitted to build a foundation for productive gardens. This mounded garden shows a form of raised bed known as hugelkultur (German for "hill culture"). Plants in hugelkultur raised beds attain mature size faster than in traditional planting beds and require very little watering.

- **Metal Gives a Modern Look**

Metal raised beds blend craftily into a contemporary style landscape. Any metal is long-lasting and carefree, and this product showcases a steel product known as Zincalume, which lasts a long time. It lasts four times as long as galvanized steel. This exact design supplies the beauty of curved edges that makes the hard look of corrugated metal become softer.

- **Aim High With Beds**

Tall raised beds can cause a small yard look larger by injecting vertical interest. Taller beds take the backache out of plant maintenance that is going on by getting rid of the stooping necessary to tend in-ground beds. While building taller beds, try to add simple benches that make use of the raised beds as a backrest.

- **Grow Up in Raised Beds**

Use the frame of a raised bed to make a construction platform to host a trellis, and you can fill your garden with climbing flowers or foods, such as snow peas. The frame of a raised bed supplies multiple choices for attaching accessory items, such as a floating row cover, frost blanket or mesh fencing to frighten animals.

- **Box Your Garden**

Extra-large red cedar boxes let you build a custom raised bed garden design. Five boxes of different sizes come as part of a set. Assemble the planter boxes in a design that makes good use of your growing region, sunlight or yard shape. Long-lasting cedar is rot-resistant, making it a perfect material for raised bed planters.

- **A Bed of Straw**

With straw bales, build a raised bed that's fully compostable. Straw beds supply a host of benefits to the landscape. They are not costly and they also provide a temporary bed solution. After the garden season comes to an end, straw bales can simply be used as winter mulch or transformed into layering material for building a lasagne garden.

- **Trolley Garden Bed**

Enjoy pain-free gardening with a raised bed that is tall enough to prevent bending while tending. This high trolley garden provides an abundant 12 square feet of growing area, including a deep enough pocket to house tall crops such as tomatoes. Place shorter plants like leaf lettuce and radishes along bed edges.

Chapter 4

TOP FIVE VEGETABLES THAT GROW BEST IN RAISED BED GARDENS

The reputation and simplicity of growing vegetables in raised beds has influenced many new green thumbs to get out there and try to grow some vegetables.

Raised beds are a much loved among gardeners for many reasons. For one, the soil can be catered to your needs, because you will be filling your beds instead of using what's already available. The soil in these beds can never be stepped on, which means it never becomes compacted. This lets it drain surplus water out speedily. The soil in these beds also warms faster during springtime, providing a longer growing season.

Raised beds are great for growing nearly anything, but there are some real stars that rise higher than the rest. Let us take a look at the five best vegetables you can grow on raised beds.

- **Root vegetables**

Root vegetables are great for raised beds. Carrots, radishes, and parsnips increase in the loose, rock-free soil where they have enough space to spread out. When you're growing plants for their roots, it is vital to have total control over the soil. Raised beds can be filled up with the best soil to meet your needs; free of rocks, clay and debris that might deter the growth of roots or cause misshapen veggies.

- **Leafy greens**

Greens like lettuce, spinach and kale grow amazingly in raised beds. These cool weather crops have to be planted just the instant you get a trowel into your soil. The fact that soil in raised beds warms much faster than the ground means you can begin earlier with these crops and get a number of great harvests before summer comes visiting.

One more reason that leafy greens are great for raised beds is they don't like soggy roots. The fast draining soil in your beds means your lovely lettuces should not stand in the water for too long.

- **Onions**

There are three reasons that onions are one of the best vegetable to grow in raised beds. They love quick draining soil, they require plenty of organic matter, and they need a long growing season. Naturally, the soil in raised beds can be catered for based on your needs, so if you are sure you will be planting onions in the bed, you can make sure you add plenty of compost. Onions grown from seeds can take more than 100 days to attain maturity. If you live somewhere with four seasons, you will want to give your onions the longest time in the garden you can handle. As stated earlier, the soil in a raised bed warms up much faster than the ground, so you can plant in advance, giving your onions a head start.

- **Tomatoes**

Tomatoes are heavy feeders that require soil full of nutrients to thrive. With a raised bed, you can customize your soil to your needs without trouble, incorporating extra compost as you fill up the beds. The only disadvantage to growing tomatoes in raised beds is that it is more difficult for tomato cages and stakes to stand up in the loose soil.

- **Potatoes**

Potatoes do not only grow perfectly in a raised bed, they are also a lot easier to harvest this way. These plants gain a lot from hilling soil around the shoots as they grow. In a raised bed, it is easy for you to contain your hills, and even build a bed that you can add as your plants grows. Potatoes require loose, loamy soil that drains very well.

They grow well when they are able to spread easily out in the soil, and this loose soil will prevent them from decaying. In a raised bed, you have the advantage of total control over the soil. Potato crops grown in raised beds are likely to have higher yields with bigger tubers.

These are just few of the crops that can grow well in a raised bed. These are some the crops that can grow easily. However, with cautious planning, you can also have success with other crops. Now that you are aware of what your raised bed can do, get out there and get your hands working!

Chapter 5

TIPS FOR RAISED BED GARDENING

Raised beds are awesome: the soil in the beds warms and dries out earlier in the spring than usual garden beds, so you can start planting sooner. They allow you to garden without fighting stones and roots, and the soil in them stays flawlessly fluffy because it doesn't get walked on.

Of course, there are a few disadvantages: in hot dry weather, raised beds may begin to dry out quickly. Roots from close by trees will eventually find their way into your fine, nutrient-dense soil.

Roaming cats may also find the nice, fluffy soil perfect for their own reasons. However, these few negative aspects are easy to evade with a little planning and prevention.

TEN TIPS FOR RAISED BED GARDENING

- **Don't ever -- ever! -- walk on the soil**

The biggest benefit of raised bed gardening is the light, fluffy, perfect soil which you can work with. When you construct your raised beds, design them so that you're able to get to every part of the bed without the need to stand in it. If you already have a raised bed and discover that you have to walk on parts of it, try installing strategically placed patio pavers or boards, and only step on that instead of stepping on the soil.

- **Mulch after you plant**

Mulch with straw, leaves, grass clippings, or wood chips after you have plant your garden. This will lessen the amount of weeding you will need to do and keep the soil damp.

- **Plan your irrigation system**

Two of the best methods to irrigate a raised bed are through soaker hose and drip irrigation. If you plan it before time and install your irrigation system prior to planting, you can save yourself a lot of work and time spent standing about with a hose later on.

- **Install a barrier to roots and weeds.**

If you have large trees in your area, or just want to make sure you won't have to deal with weeds growing up through your great soil, try installing a fence at the base of the bed. This could be a commercial weed barrier, a piece of used carpet, or a thick piece of corrugated cardboard. If you have an existing raised bed and find that you're dealing with tree roots every year, you may have to dig the soil, fix in the barrier, and refill with the soil. It's a bit of work, but it will save you lots of work later on.

- **Top-dress annually with compost.**

Gardening in a raised bed is, basically, like gardening in a very large container. Just like any container garden, the soil will settle and get exhausted as time goes on. You can alleviate this by adding a one or two-inch layer of compost or composted manure every spring prior to when you start planting.

- **Fluff the soil with a garden fork as needed.**

To ease compacted soil in your raised bed, just drive a garden fork deep down into the soil, as deeply as you can, and twist it back and forth. Do that at eight to twelve-inch intervals all around the bed and your soil will be perfectly loosened without tons of backbreaking work.

- **Cover up your soil, even when you're not gardening.**

Add a layer of organic mulch or plant a cover crop as your growing season ends. Soil that is out in the open to harsh winter weather breaks down and compacts quicker than soil that is protected.

- **Plant annual cover crops.**

Annual cover crops, like annual ryegrass, crimson clover, and hairy vetch, sowed at the end of the growing season, will supply many benefits to your raised bed garden. They give nutrients to the soil (particularly if you dig them into the bed in spring), decrease erosion, and (in the case of vetch and clover) transport nitrogen in your soil.

- **Think ahead to lengthen the season.**

A little planning can allow you to grow earlier in the season or lengthen your growing season well into the fall. Try installing supports for an easy low tunnel or cold frame, and you'll have little work when you need to shield your crops from frost!

- **Consider composting directly in your raised bed garden.**

Worm tubes, trench composting, and dig-and-drop composting are all techniques you can use to compost straight in your raised bed garden. You will be able to enhance your soil without ever needing to turn a compost pile.

How Many Raised Beds Can You Have?

The number of raised beds you can have is restricted only by your budget and is determined by what you want. If you are a homesteader looking for food self-sufficiency, a rough guide is 700 square feet of planting space per individual.

A market gardener would make use of even more space. If you build beds 4 feet wide by 25 feet long, that would mean seven raised beds per member of the family. For raised beds that measure, 4 feet wide by 8 feet long (a very normal size) that would be 22 beds per individual.

That is however a very rough guideline. Now you can see that if you want to use raised beds to grow food in a large quantity, you will need to build quite a few of them! Don't feel frightened. You can add a few more raised beds every season and keep on growing crops in the ground in the period in-between.

However, if raised beds are your only option for growing, just invest in time, labor, and money, and benefit from the rewards for many seasons. The tip is to construct beds for the next season in the summer or fall, not in the spring. Plant a cover crop for in the winter.

When spring comes, you can cut the cover crops and put them into the compost, cultivate the accessible soil in the beds, and plant.

You have picked your material, your site, and the number of beds you will build. Now there is nothing left but to actually start creating the beds!

Chapter 6

BENEFITS OF RAISED BED GARDENING

Raised bed gardening is not a new idea. Traditional gardeners used to double dig their beds to form rectangular or circular mounds 1-1 ½ ft. high, with sloping edges. A typical practice in areas that gets plenty of rain, it ensured good drainage, besides providing a bit of extra space for growing vegetables.

This form of gardening also showed itself to be ideal for many companion plantings such as carrots and onion family vegetables. The carrots went on the flat top of the beds and enjoyed the deep soil while the onions and leeks planted on the sides all around kept the beds safe from pests.

Raised garden beds, also referred to as garden boxes are very good for growing small plots of vegetables and flowers. They protect your garden soil from pathway weeds, put off soil compaction, offer good drainage and they serve as an obstacle to pests like slugs and snails. The sides of the beds protect your precious garden soil from being swept by the wind or washed away during heavy rainfalls. In many regions, gardeners can plant earlier in the season since the soil is warmer and better drained when it is higher than ground level.

By elevating the soil level, raised garden beds also lessen back strain while bending over to take care of the bed. This is particularly helpful to elderly gardeners or people who have bad backs. And if the beds are well constructed, the gardener can take a seat on the frame of the bed while weeding, and for a number of gardeners, this is the greatest benefit of all.

Raised beds are not similar to garden planters. Planters are raised containers that come with bottoms to keep the soil from falling off. Planter bottoms are generally slatted, with a few type of semi-permeable cloth barrier that allows drainage. Raised beds, however, do not come with bottoms; they are open to the soil, and this offers the benefit of permitting plant roots to go further into the soil for nutrients that are available.

Raised garden beds can be found in a variety of different materials and designs, and they can be built with relative ease.

It's no surprise that contemporary gardeners are beginning to embrace the idea of raised bed gardening, albeit with a new twist. The sloping sides of the past beds have been traded for rock-hard frames that give them a well-defined look. This way, the beds can be as high as you want them to and keep soil from running off during rain.

Let's look at few of the additional benefits of raised bed gardening.

- **Good aeration**

You can build your raised beds the customary way by digging up the ground and supporting the sides with a concrete frame. Alternatively, just pile up high quality soil, decomposed farmyard manure, and compost inside the frames. Either way, it supplies the plants with an abundant growing media with a loose structure and gives room for good air circulation around the roots.

Like the other part of the plant, roots have to breathe. They breathe in the oxygen from the air and breathe out carbon dioxide. If the soil is over compacted, the roots choke and fail to grow properly. That is because good ventilation is essential for the roots to soak up essential nutrients. For instance, the air pockets in the soil grasp nitrogen that is transformed into nitrate and nitrite salts by the soil bacteria, making this macronutrient accessible to the plant. Fewer air pockets mean less nitrogen will be available.

Proper ventilation is vital for keeping the microbial population in the soil healthy. It helps keep up a balance between the aerobic and anaerobic bacteria that play diverse roles in improving soil fertility.

- **Good drainage**

Raised beds offer good drainage even in heavy rains. This is one of the reasons it has always been loved in tropical areas that experience heavy rainfall. The loose texture of the soil lets the water seep into the bed, keeping it from quick runoff that may carry away the fertile topsoil. At the same time, it gives room for excess water to drain away.

Nearly all plants grow healthily in moist soil, but a lot of them despise wet feet. For one thing, excess water around the roots disturbs their breathing. In addition, regular moisture allows bacterial and fungal diseases. Water logging can even alter the pH of the soil, making it more acidic and less favourable to plants preferring neutral to faintly alkaline soils.

The perfect soil moisture for nearly all plants is about 25%, even though bog plants have gotten used to living in soils saturated with water. When you water your plants growing in raised beds, the water is absorbed into the lower layers of the beds rather quickly. It keeps the soil uniformly moist but without letting the water to stagnate.

- **Root spread**

It is obvious that plant roots would find it easier to grow and spread in all directions when the soil is loose. Not only that but, the framed beds preserve moisture much longer than the conventional raised beds because water loss from the sides is reduced. This prevents the beds from drying out between watering and facilitates good root run.

Plants that are growing in the ground generally have a shallow root system except the ground is tilled deep before planting. Such plants are not able to access the moisture in the lower layers of soil, and are more likely to become dehydrated as soon as the surface moisture evaporates. A well-developed root system secures the plant and helps it collect water and nutrients from a bigger area that is mostly important for vegetables. They have to grow strongly and produce utmost yield within a short period.

- **Less risk of soil compaction**

Raised bed planting may not stop your cats and dogs from playing in the mud and digging up the soil, but there is little chance of people and larger animals carelessly walking on the beds and tamping down the soil. If the width of the beds is left at 3-4 feet, you can carry out other gardening chores such as fertilizing, weeding and harvesting without walking on the bed.

Flooding during rains is an additional way the soil in cultivated fields becomes compacted. The wet and heavy soil particles settle down, filling the air spaces. While the water evaporates, it leaves behind a solid and dense layer of soil, making it less welcoming to plants. With water rapidly draining away from raised planting beds, there is no hazard of soil compaction caused by flooding.

- **Better weed control**

Raised beds come upon relatively little weed problems. Even if you double dig the ground and thoroughly remove all the weeds, you might notice weeds taking over the beds soon enough.

The deep cultivation shows many weed seeds lying inactive in the soil. Sun exposure and the added water they get when you irrigate the field offer them the long-awaited chance to sprout. They hurriedly take root in the fertile soil and bloom on the nutrients meant for your plants.

When building the raised beds, you have the option of filling the frames with compost and soil quite free of weeds. The loose soil and good ease of access to the beds make it easier to pull up the few weeds that may show up. In addition, the universal practice is to position plants very close to each other. When they grow and fill in the bed, they do an outstanding job of choking out weeds.

Conclusion

Raised beds are almost very easy to build and even easier to maintain. They are an easy way to get into gardening. It is great for both small-scale home gardeners and for mild large-scale production.

Whether you purchase your raised garden beds or you build yours, you will surely reap many benefits from raised bed gardening.

There are different types and designs of raised bed, you can simply choose the one that suits your needs and you can have more than one raised garden bed.

STEVE MUFIA

If you enjoyed this book or benefited from it in any way, then I would greatly appreciate if you would be kind enough to leave a review for this book on Amazon.

Please click below link to leave a review on Amazon.com.

https://www.amazon.com/review/
create-review?asin=B0797MYX5C#

Thank You.

Check Out Other Books

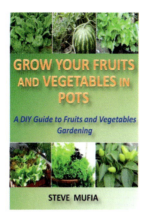

https://www.amazon.com/dp/B075KT2W5G/

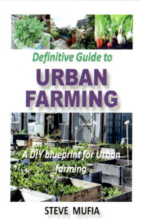

https://www.amazon.com/dp/B0778T8VZL/

Printed in Poland
by Amazon Fulfillment
Poland Sp. z o.o., Wrocław